91st U.S. Open
Hazeltine National Golf Club

Writer
John Hopkins

Photographers
Lawrence Levy
Rusty Jarrett

Editor
Bev Norwood

ISBN 1-878843-02-8

©1991 United States Golf Association®
Golf House, Far Hills, New Jersey 07931

Statistics produced by Unisys Corporation

Published by International Merchandising Corporation,
One Erieview Plaza, Cleveland, Ohio 44114

Designed and produced by Davis Design

Printed in the United States of America

91st
U.S. Open
Official Annual Presented by
ROLEX

The new U.S. Open champion is a golfer whom I have watched closely for most of his professional career. Payne Stewart has made his home for quite a while in Orlando, Florida, at the Bay Hill Club, where I have been associated for more than 20 years.

Payne enjoys Bay Hill for the same reason I do. There we're both just two of the guys, along with a few other Tour players and amateurs of various skill levels. We enjoy playing golf together, relaxing and being ourselves. Payne is popular there, a likeable person with an excellent golf game. We all suffered with him in his defeats while he matured as a player, and celebrated his triumphs.

Obviously, we were elated when Payne won the U.S. Open, although I personally can empathize with him and with Scott Simpson, whom he beat in the playoff, since I won one U.S. Open in regulation holes and lost three times in playoffs, once after giving up a lead that I never should have lost.

This is the seventh annual commemorative book on the U.S. Open, presented by our friends at Rolex. The purpose of this book is two-fold—to provide a record in words and color photographs of the U.S. Open, and to promote junior golf through the sales proceeds of the book. All proceeds are directed to the USGA Associates Program and are designated for activities to benefit junior golf.

In that regard, it was perhaps appropriate that the USGA Junior Amateur Championship was scheduled for the Bay Hill Club in 1991, the same year that a member of our club won the U.S. Open.

Arnold Palmer

Arnold Palmer

91st U.S. Open

June 13-17, 1991, Hazeltine National Golf Club, Chaska, Minnesota

Contestant	Rounds				Total	Prize
Payne Stewart	67	70	73	72	282	$235,000.00
Scott Simpson	70	68	72	72	282	117,500.00
(Stewart won playoff, 75 to 77)						
Larry Nelson	73	72	72	68	285	62,574.00
Fred Couples	70	70	75	70	285	62,574.00
Fuzzy Zoeller	72	73	74	67	286	41,542.00
Scott Hoch	69	71	74	73	287	36,090.00
Nolan Henke	67	71	77	73	288	32,176.00
Raymond Floyd	73	72	76	68	289	26,958.33
Jose Maria Olazabal	73	71	75	70	289	26,958.33
Corey Pavin	71	67	79	72	289	26,958.33
D.A. Weibring	76	71	75	68	290	20,909.20
Davis Love III	70	76	73	71	290	20,909.20
Jim Gallagher, Jr.	70	72	75	73	290	20,909.20
Craig Parry	70	73	73	74	290	20,909.20
Hale Irwin	71	75	70	74	290	20,909.20
Tom Watson	73	71	77	70	291	17,186.00
Nick Faldo	72	74	73	72	291	17,186.00
Sandy Lyle	72	70	74	75	291	17,186.00
Billy Ray Brown	73	71	77	71	292	14,166.57
Peter Persons	70	75	75	72	292	14,166.57
Mark Brooks	73	73	73	73	292	14,166.57
Tom Sieckmann	74	70	74	74	292	14,166.57
John Cook	76	70	72	74	292	14,166.57
Craig Stadler	71	69	77	75	292	14,166.57
Nick Price	74	69	71	78	292	14,166.57
Tim Simpson	73	72	76	72	293	11,711.60
Mike Reid	74	72	74	73	293	11,711.60
Bob Tway	75	69	75	74	293	11,711.60
Jodie Mudd	71	70	77	75	293	11,711.60
Rick Fehr	74	69	73	77	293	11,711.60
Dave Rummells	72	73	77	72	294	10,133.17
Edward Humenik	72	70	78	74	294	10,133.17
Christopher Perry	72	73	75	74	294	10,133.17
Peter Jacobsen	72	73	74	75	294	10,133.17
Lance Ten Broeck	72	73	74	75	294	10,133.17
Brian Kamm	69	73	73	79	294	10,133.17
Tom Purtzer	77	68	77	73	295	8,560.43
Mark Calcavecchia	69	74	78	74	295	8,560.43
Billy Mayfair	72	73	76	74	295	8,560.43
Keith Clearwater	70	76	74	75	295	8,560.43
Tom Kite	71	75	74	75	295	8,560.43
Buddy Gardner	74	72	74	75	295	8,560.43
Andy North	71	71	77	76	295	8,560.43
Ian Baker-Finch	77	70	75	74	296	7,477.50
Jim Hallet	72	74	73	77	296	7,477.50
Rodger Davis	74	68	81	74	297	6,875.67
Jack Nicklaus	70	76	77	74	297	6,875.67

Contestant	Rounds				Total	Prize
Blaine McCallister	72	72	76	77	297	6,875.67
Steve Pate	72	75	77	74	298	6,033.75
Michael Harwood	71	74	77	76	298	6,033.75
Wayne Levi	72	72	76	78	298	6,033.75
Loren Roberts	75	70	74	79	298	6,033.75
Larry Rinker	72	72	77	78	299	5,389.00
John Inman	72	72	77	78	299	5,389.00
*Phil Mickelson	73	72	80	75	300	Medal
Larry Mize	73	73	79	75	300	5,164.50
Steve Gotsche	72	75	76	77	300	5,164.50
Steve Elkington	77	69	76	78	300	5,164.50
Ian Woosnam	73	68	79	80	300	5,164.50
David Graham	74	71	80	77	302	5,008.00
Stan Utley	73	71	81	78	303	4,958.00
John Adams	72	75	78	79	304	4,958.00
Terry Snodgrass	74	73	80	78	305	4,958.00
Lanny Wadkins	76	70	80	79	305	4,958.00
Wayne Grady	73	74	78	80	305	4,958.00

Tom Byrum	68-80—148	Scott Gump	77-73—150	Bob Lasken	81-74—155
Jeff Sluman	75-73—148	Tom Tolles	74-77—151	Ed Dougherty	79-76—155
Paul Azinger	72-76—148	Bill Britton	73-78—151	Brad Faxon	79-76—155
Bob Estes	72-76—148	Rick Price	77-74—151	Eric Booker	78-77—155
Eric Johnson	77-71—148	David Jackson	70-81—151	John Ross	77-79—156
Lee Janzen	74-74—148	Dan Halldorson	76-75—151	Brian Tennyson	77-79—156
Fulton Allem	71-78—149	Fred Funk	75-76—151	Cary Hungate	77-79—156
Mark McCumber	76-73—149	Billy Andrade	76-75—151	Jacob Ferenz	75-82—157
Bernhard Langer	75-74—149	Rocco Mediate	77-74—151	Jay Gunning	83-74—157
Seve Ballesteros	72-77—149	Curtis Strange	77-74—151	John Paesani	82-75—157
Timothy Robyn	79-70—149	Bobby Wadkins	75-76—151	Jeb Stuart	78-79—157
Jon Chaffee	74-75—149	Billy Tuten	75-76—151	*Jeff Lee	80-78—158
Frank Dobbs	73-76—149	*Chris Gorgone	76-75—151	Scott Beaugureau	81-77—158
John Huston	72-77—149	Dennis Zinkon	78-73—151	Sam Randolph	81-78—159
David Frost	75-74—149	Jerry Pate	78-74—152	Rick Vershure	79-80—159
Lee Trevino	77-72—149	Rocky Walcher	76-76—152	Michael Weeks	79-80—159
Mark O'Meara	73-76—149	Steve Jones	76-76—152	James Detrixhe	80-80—160
Gil Morgan	76-73—149	Jumbo Ozaki	77-75—152	Louie Garcia	82-78—160
Jay Delsing	74-75—149	Chip Beck	75-77—152	Darrell Kestner	78-83—161
Mitch Adcock	79-70—149	Jerry Foltz	77-76—153	Terry Dear	83-78—161
Tom Eubank	75-74—149	Andrew Magee	74-79—153	Jack Kay, Jr.	79-83—162
Robert Meyer	76-74—150	Ray Stewart	77-76—153	Clay Devers	81-81—162
Jim Benepe	74-76—150	Jon Hough	76-77—153	Joe Hajduch	88-75—163
Mike Donald	74-76—150	Phil Blackmar	77-76—153	Chris Endres	85-80—165
John Wilson	78-72—150	Jay Overton	81-73—154	Paul Oglesby	86-81—167
Brad Sherfy	78-72—150	Richard Osberg	73-81—154	George Daves	82-85—167
Kirk Triplett	75-75—150	Jim McGovern	77-77—154	Greg Norman	78 WD
*Allen Doyle	76-74—150	Bruce Zabriski	83-71—154	Ronan Rafferty	79 WD
Hal Sutton	77-73—150	Robert Gamez	76-78—154	Ken Green	81 WD
Dave Barr	76-74—150	Dicky Thompson	75-79—154		
Bob Boyd	75-75—150	Bryan Norton	78-77—155		

Professionals not returning 72-hole scores received $1,000 each.   *Denotes amateur.

Men with eight-syllable names cut a wide swathe through the avenues of life. Totten Peavey Heffelfinger did. An uncle was Pudge Heffelfinger, the great Yale football player. Another relative founded Peavey & Co., a vast grain concern in Minneapolis. From early on, Tot Heffelfinger became accustomed to having his own way, and not just because of his imposing physical presence. He stood well over six feet and weighed 225 pounds, and his character was, how shall we say, strong.

In Minneapolis in the mid-1950s, men like Heffelfinger were members of the Minikahda Club, a stately enclave of old money and new sports. Members of Minikahda played golf by the rules. To consider an infringement was unheard of, especially by Tot, a member of the Royal and Ancient Golf Club of St. Andrews and president of the United States Golf Association in 1952 and 1953. Tot was playing golf with his son, Mark, one day, a friendly father-and-son game, when Mark's ball rolled under a pine tree.

"I'm just going to kick this ball out, Dad," said Mark.

"If you do, that will be a two-stroke penalty," said Tot.

About this time, Heffelfinger began to think about bringing a major championship to Minnesota. Chick Evans had won the 1916 U.S. Open, which had been staged at his club, and Bobby Jones had won the 1930 U.S. Open at Interlachen en route to his Impregnable Quadrilateral, or Grand Slam. Tot wanted more.

First, though, he needed a course, be- cause his beloved Minikahda was nearly 60 years old and experiencing growing pains. Water was getting low; the suburbs of Minneapolis were encroaching; a new expressway threatened to cut through the course. It was time to expand.

Club officials took an option on a parcel of land near Chaska, a town 25 miles southwest of Minneapolis.

At first, Heffelfinger proposed that the club have two courses, but the members voted this down. Heffelfinger went ahead anyway, drawing in his friends to help. One of them brought along a middle-aged golf course architect, a fellow by the name of Jones—Robert Trent Jones.

One afternoon in 1959, while the PGA Championship was being played at the Minneapolis Golf Club, Heffelfinger led a convoy of his friends and business associates to the site of the new property. Jones looked around and liked what he saw: fields of alfalfa and corn bounded by woods. Here and there water glinted in the summer sunshine.

"If you can't build a beautiful course here with the hills, woods and the lake, then you shouldn't be in the business," he said.

It was first named the Executive Golf Club of Minnesota, later changed to Hazeltine National Golf Club. From the start, Hazeltine was to be a golf club, not a country club. No swimming pool. Only a few tennis courts. Not many carts, and use of them was frowned on. An excellent junior program.

Hazeltine cost one million dollars to build. It staged its first championship four years after it opened. The 1966 U.S. Women's Open was followed by the Minnesota Golf Classic, a PGA Tour event, in

Spectators were in abundance from the first practice day onwards.

The No. 3 fairway slopes left to right, towards trees that guard the approach from the right side.

1967. By then Heffelfinger's influence had secured the 1970 U.S. Open for Hazeltine. Club officials didn't know what they were letting themselves in for.

The first signs of trouble arose when an article under Jack Nicklaus' name, headlined "Blind Man's Bluff," appeared in *Sports Illustrated* before the Open. "What really sets the course apart is a factor I call lack of definition," Nicklaus wrote. "On most courses a player has a pretty definite sense of where he is going even if he can't see the pin from the tee. At Hazeltine the topography on the majority of holes does not establish a frame for the golfer. ... On several tees I did not have a clue as to which direction the hole might be. I thought then that many players will need tour guides as well as caddies in this Open.

"Instead of playing their drives at some visual marker on the hole, the golfers will be forced instead to aim their tee shots at things like barns or water towers. Then on the 18th you aim for the left chimney of Tot Heffelfinger's roof. The right chimney probably leads to Winnipeg."

At this stage in his career, Jones had a thing about doglegs. Ten of the 14 driving holes were doglegs, many of them severe. "These (dogleg) holes demand short, precise drives to position A ... there is no position B," Nicklaus said. There were so many dogleg holes it wasn't possible to find one on which to measure the length of the pros' drives.

After the second round of the 1970 U.S. Open, Dave Hill was asked for his comments about the course. Hill, who had been drinking with friends and by his own count had consumed five vodka and orange drinks, didn't hold back. He said, among other things, that the architect must have had his plans upside down, that when the course was built it ruined a perfectly good farm, and somebody ought to plow it up so a good course could be built on it. Asked what the course lacked, Hill responded, "Eighty acres of corn and a few cows." For these comments Hill was fined $150 by the then PGA Tour Commissioner Joe Dey.

Two voices were not raised in anger about the course. One belonged to Dan Jenkins. "The pros don't like any hole with a tree, a pond, or a par five that can't be reached with a drive and a swizzle stick," he wrote in *Sports Illustrated*. He saw nothing wrong in being able to see a barn from the first hole. "The Open had come to the Midwest. Well, here was a hole that said, 'Welcome to the Midwest.' All courses don't look like Augusta National, and they shouldn't."

The other voice that found no reason to speak out against the course was that of Tony Jacklin, and the reason was he was playing some of the best golf of his life. The young Englishman, the reigning British Open champion, led by two strokes after the first round, three after 36 holes, four after 54 holes and by seven at the end. It was the biggest margin of victory for 49 years. Rounds of 71, 70, 70 and 70 gave him a total of 281, seven under par. He was the only player under par at the finish.

Changes had to be made and made they were, though Tot Heffelfinger didn't like it. "They're leading us by the damn nose," he said with all the hauteur he could muster, which was considerable. Robert Trent Jones returned soon after the 1970 Open and made some modifications. Coming back again, he made even further revisions, completely redesigning both the 16th and 17th holes and straightening many of the doglegs.

Then, in 1987, Rees Jones, son of Robert

The 166-yard No. 8 is the shortest hole on the course, but water guards the green and there are bunkers on the back and left.

Trent, was approached by Reed Mackenzie, the 1991 U.S. Open's General Chairman, and asked to rework Hazeltine. Rees Jones' excellent work in remodeling The Country Club at Brookline, Massachusetts, for the 1988 U.S. Open had been noticed.

"The most frequent task in remodeling is the addition of definition which can roughly be explained as the revelation by the course and its features of the shot that is required," Rees explained. "Why is definition needed? Because with the modern popularity of the game, there are so many more players out there and you must make the course assist their pace of play, keep them moving. So much of my independent experience in golf course architecture has involved remodeling. I think that's why they called me in to touch up Hazeltine, because I have become known as the architect of definition."

If Jacklin had returned this year, he would scarcely have recognized the site of his great conquest. Fourteen holes had undergone major alterations. Rees Jones turned the 16th, formerly a long par three along Lake Hazeltine, into a 384-yard par four with a creek added along the left side. The 17th, a short par four, became a strong par three. And the 18th, which had been a vicious dogleg, was straightened. Now it's a 452-yard uphill test. Only the fourth, sixth, 12th, and 15th remain as they were 21 years ago.

Additionally, all the greens were stripped after being struck by a blight in 1985. They were re-sodded with Pencross bentgrass.

"They should be fairly consistent because the grass is all of the same generation," Rees

The approach on the par-four 16th hole is a dogleg right to a green that juts out as a peninsula.

Ponds guard the left and front right of the green at No. 17, a par three of 182 yards.

Jones said. "Also, when they stripped the greens, they took out some of the abruptness of their contours. There won't be any severely pitched greens like the 17th at Medinah or the fifth at The Country Club."

The final touches to the course were brought about by the weather. After weeks of heavy rain—four inches fell in 10 hours one day before the Open began—the course was sodden, waterlogged in parts. Helicopters were brought in and hovered over the course to create a drying downdraft. Mercifully, the sun began to shine then, and the result was the course was transformed in a few days.

The reaction of the players when they arrived at Hazeltine made them sound like cats who had stumbled on saucers of cream.

Tom Watson: "You can have a wonderful time on this course. It may be the best Open course I have ever played. This is a great course and it should determine a great champion."

Seve Ballesteros: "It is a challenging course and the way it is set up is, in my opinion, how it should be. I think it is fair."

Curtis Strange: "In 1970 I saw and read everything that was said and I didn't know what to expect coming here. It is a fair course and it should be a lot of fun playing it."

Nick Faldo: "The course is good, very straightforward, an honest test of golf. No tricks, no surprises. It is one of the best U.S. Open courses we have seen—perfect."

Even the man who started all the fuss was moved to praise the changes. "It's totally different," Dave Hill said. "It has grown into a lovely course. It has maturity and definition. I am sure they will have a great Open."

The U.S. Open falls at a perfect time of the year to pause and take stock. Mid-June, mid-season, 23 events played on the PGA Tour, 29 more to come.

As we all gathered in Minnesota for the 91st U.S. Open, it seemed an appropriate moment to ask two questions. The first: Why couldn't Europeans win the Open? Hazeltine in 1991 marked a famous anniversary for Europeans because 21 years earlier Tony Jacklin had run away with the Open there. It was the last success in this event by a European.

It's not as if the Europeans hadn't won anything else. Started by Jacklin and then inspired by Seve Ballesteros, European golf strode into a golden era in the years from 1971 to the present. European golfers have won seven of the past 12 Masters, not lost a Ryder Cup since 1983 and allowed an American victory in the British Open only once in the past seven years.

No U.S. Opens, however.

Nick Faldo came close in 1988, only losing in a playoff to Curtis Strange. Faldo missed getting into another playoff last year by half the width of a golf ball. Ian Woosnam gave it a go at Rochester in 1989, tying for second.

What all this adds up to is that Jacklin is the only European player to have won the U.S. Open since the end of the Second World War.

Why?

Does the USGA set up the Open courses in such a way that the Europeans can't cope with them? Hardly. There are dozens of golfers who can't cope with a U.S. Open course. Most of them are Americans. "It's not as if the Americans play under the conditions (of a U.S. Open) any more than we do," said Nick Faldo. He laughed. "They're as confused as we are."

A more obvious reason is the imbalance of the numbers. One hundred and fifty-six men will tee off on Thursday; seven will be Europeans. For such small numbers they carried an impressive amount of firepower. Ballesteros, Faldo, Woosnam, Sandy Lyle and Bernhard Langer were past or present Masters champions, Ballesteros and Faldo twice. Ballesteros, Lyle and Faldo were past or present British Open champions, Ballesteros and Faldo two or more times. Woosnam was having a dream year, and Ballesteros had emerged as a major contender from a major slump.

"It's time there was a European victory," said Tony Jacklin on the eve of the Open. "I'd like to think there will be one this year, and it must help the lads to know that the last person to win there was old T.J. But the Europeans are outnumbered by what, seven to one, ten to one, twenty to one?"

Second question: Where have the American superstars gone? "The well-known personalities responsible for the game's popularity—Arnold Palmer, Jack Nicklaus, Lee Trevino—have been replaced by a mob of marvelous but obscure golfing robots," wrote Curt Brown in the Minneapolis *Star Tribune*.

So obscure that Hale Irwin was moved to remark of one of the PGA Tour's most successful players this year: "I dare say there weren't too many of us a while back who knew who or what Rocco Mediate was," said the defending champion, who

Great friends and rivals, Greg Norman (left) and Masters champion Ian Woosnam were among the favorites entering the U.S. Open.

had given 45-year-old men an enormous charge of pleasure by his victory at Medinah in 1990. "It might have been an embalming fluid."

You could put it another way and Rick Reilly did. Writing in *Sports Illustrated* he asked: "Quick, what do Nolan Henke, Jay Don Blake, Ted Schulz, Rocco Mediate, Andrew Magee, Larry Silveira, Mark Brooks and Kenny Perry have in common?

(a) They play for the Barcelona Dragons of the WLAF.

(b) They are Lotto winners.

(c) They are members of Winners Anonymous, the self-help group of good players and near goods who have won golf tournaments this year to deafening quiet.

The answer is (c) touring pros who have cashed a winner's check in 1991, yet still need IDs to get a bucket of balls at the practice range."

"We're so evenly matched it's getting like auto racing out there," said Tim Simpson. "There's one mile an hour between us and whoever gets hot with the putter and gets a couple of breaks, wins." This evenness was borne out by the fact that there were 18 different winners on the first 20 events this year.

But just a minute. Those were tournaments which men like Corey Pavin and Billy Andrade had won two of already this year. What I am talking about now is the U.S. Open, the most prestigious event anyone can win, the national championship of the game's leading country.

The following names aren't fly-by-nights, men who come one week, are gone the next: Tom Watson, Fuzzy Zoeller, Larry Nelson, Raymond Floyd, Curtis Strange and Irwin. Between them these men have won 10 U.S. Opens and 22 major titles. They are genuine world stars, men with long entries in record books, men who are looked up to by their peers. They bear out my point that whatever else may happen, the U.S. Open produces worthy winners.

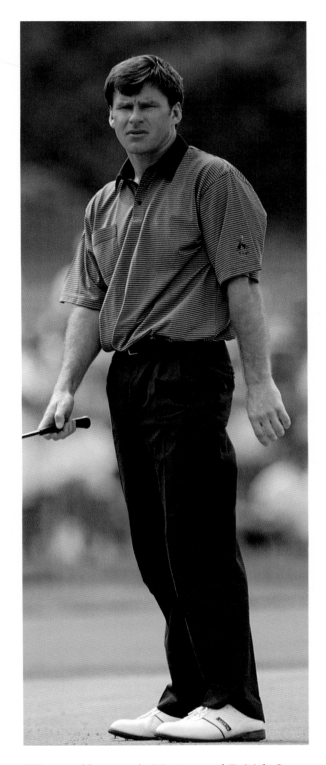

Out of the doldrums, Seve Ballesteros (opposite) had won three tournaments in his last five starts before the U.S. Open.

Winner of last year's Masters and British Open, Nick Faldo led the European contingent at Hazeltine.

During the night of June 12th there was a severe thunderstorm. It wasn't the rain that pattered against the windows of my hotel room that woke me because the windows were double-glazed. It was the flashes of lightning and the rumble of thunder. I looked at my watch. It was 4 a.m. A wet Open, I thought in my half awake, half asleep state.

Sandy Tatum is often quoted as saying about a U.S. Open: "We're not trying to embarrass the best players, we are merely trying to identify them." The Open always has, and as it drew close this year, I suspected it would again.

I had a hunch the winner might be a European, Jose Maria Olazabal, or Faldo perhaps, but I felt sure if it wasn't, then it would be an American of the highest class, one of whom it could be said confidently and loudly, of whom it would ring absolutely true: "Ladies and gentlemen, the U.S. Open champion."

Wasn't I right? Rain and all.

Corey Pavin had won twice in 1991, and was the current leader of the PGA Tour's money list.

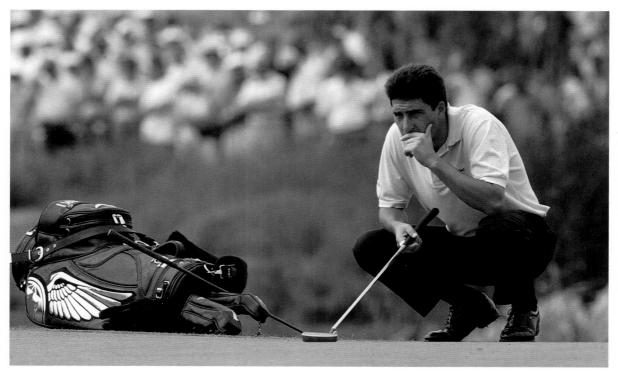

Billy Andrade (opposite page) had two successive victories en route to Hazeltine, but would miss the 36-hole cut. Many regard Jose Maria Olazabal (above) as the best young (age 25) golfer in the world.

17

A tragedy occurred today, the first day. A fierce storm hit Hazeltine National soon after midday. One spectator was killed and five others were injured when lightning struck just after 1 p.m.

There had been a thunderstorm during the night and soon after dawn it looked as though *The Old Farmers' Almanac* was right when it said that the peak of Minnesota's rainy season occurs on June 13th, today.

By 9:00 a.m. it was overcast and steamy. By midday the wind had risen and the sky darkened. At 12:49 play was suspended after bolts of lightning were seen.

Players sought refuge where they could. Nick Faldo, Hale Irwin, Phil Mickelson, and later Tom Watson sheltered in a green-keepers' storage shed by the side of the 12th tee alongside several hundred pounds of fertilizer. Scott Hoch, Nolan Henke and their wives sheltered in a van

It was a tragic day, despite the weather warnings.

near the 11th tee. Officials posted storm warning signs.

Still, the wind rose. Rain began to fall very heavily. At 1:07 a willow tree between the 11th and 16th fairways was struck by lightning. Bark was ripped off the trunk in two places and six spectators who were huddling under the tree were hit.

Witnesses said they heard two or three booms and a crackle of lightning and then saw a brilliant flash. After the victims had fallen to the ground, witnesses seemed momentarily stunned by what they had seen. "It looked like bowling pins falling over," said Greg Groom of Minnetonka. "I was not sure if they were dodging the lightning or fell to the ground."

One victim described it thus: "All of a sudden, bang! and I felt this jolt. My legs went totally numb and I was down. I've never felt anything like that before in my life. I would imagine what it was like if you were shot. My legs felt they were 50 feet wide."

The six were treated by doctors and

Nolan Henke (opposite) was four under par on the first nine en route to a 67 in the first round.

19

nurses within a minute or so after the strike, and then taken to a hospital. Five recovered, but William Fadell, 27, of Spring Park, who had suffered cardiac arrest, never regained consciousness and died at the St. Francis Regional Hospital, in Shakopee, a small town near Chaska.

Speaking at a televised press conference, David Fay, the USGA's executive director, said, "It is a tragic situation. Something like this is the nightmare you hope you don't have in golf administration. You can deal fairly effectively with the players, but if you have 40,000 people in an open space, it is not an exact science to get them to safe areas. There is no central evacuation place for them to go to. It's times like this, you wish golf was played in a domed stadium."

It was only the third fatality in almost

First Round

Nolan Henke	67	-5
Payne Stewart	67	-5
Tom Byrum	68	-4
Scott Hoch	69	-3
Mark Calcavecchia	69	-3
Brian Kamm	69	-3
Keith Clearwater	70	-2
Jim Gallagher, Jr.	70	-2
Jack Nicklaus	70	-2
Fred Couples	70	-2
Peter Persons	70	-2
David Jackson	70	-2
Craig Parry	70	-2
Davis Love III	70	-2
Scott Simpson	70	-2

Professional Terry Dear of Lubbock, Texas, struck the first shot at 7 a.m.

100 years of USGA events. In 1983, Robert Grant died of cardiac arrest while playing the first hole at Hazeltine National during the U.S. Senior Open. Back in 1922, a spectator at the Public Links championship strolled into the woods and shot himself.

The storm altered the playing conditions between the morning and afternoon rounds. Twenty-four players had completed their rounds when play was halted. Their average score was 76.002. When the average of the day was calculated it came to 74.898. There were five sub-70 rounds; all shot by afternoon players.

Curtis Strange, Rocco Mediate, and Hal Sutton shot 77s after teeing off between 9:00 a.m. and 9:30 a.m. But by the end of the day the leaders were Payne Stewart and Henke, both at 67, Tom Byrum, 68, and

Hoch and Mark Calcavecchia, both on 69. Three of them—Byrum, Hoch and Henke—had started by the time the storm hit and Byrum, who had gone the furthest, was on the fifth tee.

Play resumed at 3:30, and Stewart, who was due off at 1:30, started his round at 4:00. Having complained of back pain the previous day, he wore his brace today beneath clothes colored the bright purple and yellow of the Minnesota Vikings. And he felt better.

Stewart was the only man in the entire field not to have a bogey. He began with three birdies in the first four holes. "I hit 16 greens and 10 fairways," Stewart said, "Obviously I'm excited with the way I played. I had a very good touch on the greens today. I never had to make a tough

Brian Kamm's 69 was the surprise of the day.

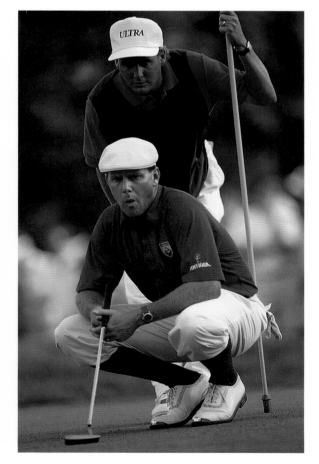

Payne Stewart shared the opening-round lead.

21

comebacker. I'm excited. I had a lot of poise and confidence, and it produced a 67. That's a nice way to start an Open."

All Henke wanted to do in his second U.S. Open was to play well enough to be around on Sunday. Then he could go fishing in Alaska with a clear conscience. Doesn't sound as though he had lofty aspirations, even though he had won in Phoenix in January and finished third last week. "I've never had a lot of attention, I've never needed it, never wanted it," he said.

That changed when Henke eagled the first hole, hitting a six iron 177 yards into the cup, and, "I thought, 'God, you're leading the Open. What's going on?'" Then the storm struck. After the restart, Henke carried on as he had left off, birdieing three of the next six holes to go five under par. His 32 on the first nine was the day's best score.

Byrum made a lackluster start, slipping to one over par after four holes. When play restarted, he birdied five of the remaining 14 holes. He had a ready explanation. "All of a sudden what I was doing wasn't that important," he said, thinking back to the day's fatality. "That helped take a lot of pressure off me. Maybe that is why I played so well."

Byrum made two of his birdies on two of the course's toughest holes, the 16th and 18th. He rammed in a 20-footer on the 16th and holed a 10-footer on the 18th. Hoch also birdied the same holes in his 69.

Some other odd statistics from the day. Billy Andrade, winner of the two tournaments immediately before the Open, took a triple-bogey eight on the 11th hole and a quadruple-bogey eight on the 16th. Out in 33, back in 43 made for a bizarre 76. In his 77, Strange double-bogeyed two of the four par threes, the eighth and the 13th. Lanny Wadkins double-bogeyed the par three 17th on his way to a 76. Greg Norman double-bogeyed the fifth and triple-bogeyed the eighth for a 43 on the first nine and a 78. Tom Purtzer four-putted the first for a triple-bogey seven.

Scott Hoch (opposite page) has become a consistent U.S. Open player.

Mark Calcavecchia had a good start, but that was all.

Tom Byrum shot 68, but would miss the cut.

It was a long, wet and tiring day that ended only when the remaining 33 players who hadn't completed their rounds were called in at 9:05 p.m. They would have to go out early Friday morning. Most of all, though, it was a sad day, and it took Lee Trevino, who had himself once been hit by lightning, to assess the events of the day.

"It (the death) really put a cloud over this tournament," Trevino said. "This is one of the best golf courses we ever played a U.S. Open on. The course is great, the crowds are great. This part of the country was starved for golf. It puts everything into perspective. Shooting a 77 doesn't mean a thing. How can you sit here and get frustrated by shooting a 77 when somebody died?"

Phil Mickelson (opposite page) was the only amateur to play 72 holes.

Jack Nicklaus, in his 35th consecutive Open, came home in 33 strokes for his opening 70.

When you hit 33 greens in two rounds on a course as long and demanding as Hazeltine National, then you deserve to be near the head of the field. Payne Stewart was. A 70 today put him at 137, seven under par. He led by one stroke over Nolan Henke, the other first-round leader, Corey Pavin, and Scott Simpson.

One other statistic pinpoints how well Stewart was playing from tee to green. He took 62 putts in the first two rounds. Henke took 48, Simpson 51.

Stewart had no complaints about the weather. He had gone out late on the first day, when the rain had softened the greens and the wind had died to a whisper. Today, Stewart was untroubled by the light rain showers, although they rendered much of the public parking spaces unusable.

The most successful tactic to adopt in a U.S. Open is one that reduces the margin of error to a minimum. You don't have to burn up a course as you do at almost every other tournament because you know that if you aren't, then someone else is. U.S. Open courses are laid out in such a way that their narrow fairways, ankle-high rough and fast greens demand and receive the highest respect. Practically never are they abused. To score well, you just have to hit most of the fairways from the tee and most of the greens from the fairways. That is precisely what Stewart had been doing.

"Thirty-three greens out of 36 is pretty decent," Stewart said, tipping his cap and scratching his head. "I may have played 36 holes better, but I don't remember when.

Payne Stewart (left) couldn't remember when he had played better for 36 holes, taking the lead with a 70 for a 137 total.

On target with his short game, Corey Pavin shot a 67 to share second place, one stroke behind.

I'd like to do that over the weekend."

"If he does, he'll be pretty hard to beat," said Ian Woosnam, one of his playing companions.

Stewart plotted his way around Hazeltine National's 7,149 yards as carefully as might a commanding officer in combat. He used his driver fewer times than most of his rivals, on just eight holes in the second round. On five other holes, out came the one iron. He selected his three wood once. It all seemed to be working as he hit 23 of 28 fairways in regulation figures.

"I positioned myself well off the tee, and I hit a lot of greens," Stewart said. "And I

Scott Simpson (opposite), who trailed by one stroke, is a familiar name on U.S. Open leaderboards.

Fred Couples posted two 70s for his 140 total.

Craig Stadler was three strokes off the lead.

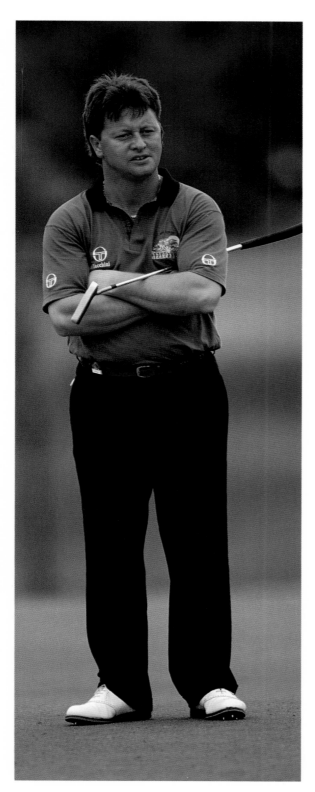

Ian Woosnam's 68 left him four strokes behind.

Second Round

Payne Stewart	70-137	-7
Nolan Henke	71-138	-6
Corey Pavin	67-138	-6
Scott Simpson	68-138	-6
Scott Hoch	71-140	-4
Fred Couples	70-140	-4
Craig Stadler	69-140	-4
Ian Woosnam	68-141	-3
Jodie Mudd	70-141	-3
Jim Gallagher, Jr.	72-142	-2
Rodger Davis	68-142	-2
Andy North	71-142	-2
Sandy Lyle	70-142	-2
Brian Kamm	73-142	-2
Ed Humenik	70-142	-2

hit a lot of good putts, although I didn't make them all. Caution was my watchword. I didn't use the driver indiscriminately. What's the point of using it on No. 15, for example? I can't get up in two and the hole is so darn long I thought I had better make sure I got there in three. I might not have done that if I had been in the rough. When you see the results, it's easier to stick to your game plan."

Stewart's round of 70 was almost without blemish. He birdied the second hole from 25 feet, the fifth from eight feet and the seventh from six feet. He parred every hole on the back nine and missed only two greens. One was the 18th and he comfortably got down in two more. The other was the short eighth, where his eight iron came up short of the green and he chipped five feet past the hole and missed the putt. It was his first bogey.

If anybody rivalled Stewart in steadiness of scoring, if not of play, then it was Simpson. Six birdies, two bogeys and a round of 68. Piece of cake.

Such steadiness was a benchmark that few could match; certainly not Scott Hoch who missed seven greens and had 10 single putts on his second nine; Corey Pavin, who shot a course-record-equalling 67 thanks to inspired putting; or Sandy Lyle, who hit only 10 fairways in two rounds and still scored 72, 70 to be only five strokes behind Stewart.

If Lyle's short game was red hot, Pavin's was molten. He chipped in from 30 feet on the second, and holed putts of 20, 8, 10, 2½ and 20 feet elsewhere. Three putts on the 17th stopped Pavin from sharing the lead with Stewart. "I've never been in contention on Open weekend before, and my idea is to go out there and not back off, not be afraid to hit the required shot," Pavin said, little knowing how those words would backfire on him 24 hours later.

Pavin also featured in one of the day's mysteries, the disappearance of Ronan Rafferty, a European Tour player. Rafferty was six over par after 24 holes and 11 over at the turn. As they walked up the ninth

Two-time Open champion Curtis Strange (77-74) missed the cut.

After rounds of 72 and 77, Seve Ballesteros also said farewell to Hazeltine.

fairway, Rafferty told Pavin and Ed Gowan, the referee, he was withdrawing. To Parry, the other member of the trio, Rafferty said, "I'm going to the toilet." He didn't reappear. It is thought that he caught a plane home to London, where several days later, his manager and the European Tour were anxious to talk to him. The Tour later fined him $8,000.

Another to withdraw, following an 81, was Ken Green.

At least Greg Norman had an excuse to withdraw. He was one under par for the first nine on Friday (although five over par overall) when he walked off the course and straight to the players' medical trailer, where he was treated for at least an hour. "I guess three straight tournaments is too

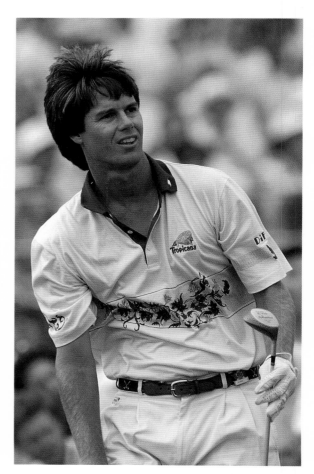

Jim Gallagher, Jr., was level par for the day and had a 142 total.

Paul Azinger (72-76) had an injured shoulder and was another victim of the cut.

many for my back," he said. Norman explained he had first felt strain in the lumbar region of his back a week earlier and revealed that the physical therapist who had been treating him all week had not wanted him to play on Friday. "I've been doing a lot of stretching exercises but not enough strengthening exercises," he said. "I will go home and rest until the British Open."

"I knew he was having a bit of trouble, but I didn't think he would walk off," said Ian Woosnam, one of Norman's playing companions, along with Stewart.

As Norman's star waned, Woosnam's waxed. After his lackluster 73 yesterday he had a 68 today. "Suddenly I can get back in this tournament," he claimed.

Backs must have been a talking point in this grouping, because Stewart moved his son out of bed in their rented house the night before—and moved into that bed himself.

"The mattress was firmer," Stewart explained. When you're leading the U.S. Open, you don't take any chances.

Phil Mickelson, the left-handed U.S. Amateur champion, made the cut again as he had at Medinah last year. He already had won a professional tournament this year, and was not in awe of his company. Mickelson's 72 outplayed Irwin's 75 and Faldo's 74.

Among the 91 who failed to make the cut was Billy Andrade, who had won the two consecutive Tour events leading up to the Open. "I guess this goes to show I'm not Superman," he said. Paul Azinger 72-76, Seve Ballesteros 72-77, Mike Donald 74-76, Curtis Strange 77-74 and Lee Trevino 77-72 were also out. Fuzzy Zoeller only made it because of a hole in one. Acing the third hole today put him two under par for 21 holes. By the end of the round he had fallen to one over par, deep among the qualifiers. "Hey, it's a four-day tournament, isn't it?" he asked.

Ten people were treated for minor cuts and bruises after a wooden stairway leading to the grandstand behind the ninth green gave way, but mercifully there was no more lightning.

Andy North posted two 71s in pursuit of a third U.S. Open title.

Jodie Mudd shot 70 and was tied for eighth place.

91st
U. S. Open
Third Round

The 16th hole at Hazeltine National is a picture-postcard-pretty par four that skirts the lake. Indian arrowheads were uncovered when the tee was being built and a creek was added when the hole was redesigned. It's a paradox. At less than 400 yards, it's the second shortest par four on the course, yet it's Hazeltine's hardest hole.

On Friday, darkness was gathering when Seve Ballesteros, Craig Stadler and Larry Mize reached the tee. The lake was as calm as a millpond. You felt you could whisper to someone across the lake, half a mile away. When they came to play their second shots to the green, they looked straight into a huge, round, setting sun. The flagstick cast a shadow longer than a sundial's.

On Saturday, though, after rain had delayed play for an hour, a wind got up. It was what Tom Watson had wanted after the calmness of the opening days, and more than he had bargained for. He shot 40-37—77. How strong was it? "Ten miles an hour," said some. "More like 20," said Hale Irwin, whose 70 was one of only two sub-par rounds all day. Nick Price's 71 was the

An even-par 72 was enough for Scott Simpson (opposite page) to gain a share of first place with Payne Stewart after three rounds. Thirty-five feet from the hole at No. 16, Stewart (above) turned a possible bogey into a dramatic par-four.

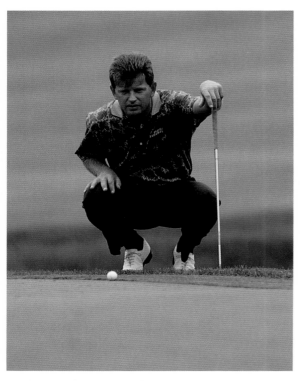

Nick Price had one of the two sub-par rounds.

other. There were three rounds of even par.

The 16th came to stand as a metaphor for the way the course had changed. The hole that yielded 32 birdies in the first two rounds gave up none to the 65 remaining competitors on Saturday as the wind rose. Its 384 yards went from a two iron and an eight iron for Jack Nicklaus to a three wood and a five iron. For the second day running, it was the hardest hole on the course with a stroke average by the 65 remaining players of 4.9 for the day. Watson and Ian Woosnam were not alone in recording sixes; Mize and Jodie Mudd took sevens, Wayne Grady, the reigning PGA champion, and Andy North took eights.

The wind had changed to the northwest and it caused the ninth, 16th, and 18th, to name but three holes, to play directly into the wind. During the first two days there were 16 rounds in the 60s; today there were none, for the first time in an Open since the first round at Shinnecock Hills in 1986. The average score was 75.669, or 3½ strokes over par.

Payne Stewart birdied the 11th with this shot, one foot from the hole, but then three-putted the 13th.

Third Round

Scott Simpson	72-210	-6
Payne Stewart	73-210	-6
Nick Price	71-214	-2
Scott Hoch	74-214	-2
Brian Kamm	73-215	-1
Fred Couples	75-215	-1
Nolan Henke	77-215	-1
Hale Irwin	70-216	E
Rick Fehr	73-216	E
Craig Parry	73-216	E
Sandy Lyle	74-216	E
Larry Nelson	72-217	+1
Jim Gallagher, Jr.	75-217	+1
Craig Stadler	77-217	+1
Corey Pavin	79-217	+1

A double bogey at No. 18 dropped Scott Hoch four strokes behind.

Fred Couples struggled to a 75 and trailed by five shots.

"I think the USGA got what they wanted today," Payne Stewart said. "From the scores, it was obvious it was the championship course it was meant to be. It was not meant to have no wind and be soft. I think every player teeing off knew it was going to be a difficult day."

Here is how the change in the weather conditions affected some of the players, their names first, then their average scores for the first two rounds followed by their third round. Ian Woosnam 70.5-79, Nolan Henke 69-77, Stadler 70-77, Raymond Floyd 72.5-76, Sandy Lyle 70-74, Corey Pavin 69-79, Jodie Mudd 70.5-77, Andy North 71-77, Watson 72-77.

The two men at the head of the field overnight coped with it almost as well as anyone. Stewart shot one-over-par 73 and Scott Simpson, 72.

Stewart started the day seven under par

Opposite, defending champion Hale Irwin (even-par 216) was in position to threaten the leaders.

Nolan Henke and his caddie had a tortuous day, finishing with a 77.

Even par for 54 holes, Sandy Lyle was regaining his championship form.

Australian Craig Parry was at even-par 216, six strokes behind.

Rick Fehr was pleased to be in the top 10 with one round left.

with a one-stroke lead over Pavin, Simpson and Henke. He birdied the third hole by rolling in an eight-foot putt, but double-bogeyed the fifth when he pulled his second shot against a leaderboard and took four strokes to reach the green. He pitched to within one foot for a birdie on the 11th, only to waste it by three-putting the 13th.

How did Stewart treat the 16th? Gingerly and a little luckily. He pulled his drive left to within inches of the creek. Then he choked down on a five iron, and chopped the ball out and into rough 20 yards in front of the green. He hit a poor chip that ended 35 feet from the flag. Just when it looked as though he was going to bogey the hole, he ran in the snakey putt.

"I was just trying to get it up there and take my medicine," said Stewart. "There was 12 inches of break on it. It was an anaconda."

Stewart closed with two more hard-won pars. Playing into the wind on the 18th, he needed to use his driver from the tee and again from the fairway, and having reached the green, he used the toe of his putter, as he did on several other occasions, to putt his ball from the fringe where it was resting against longer grass.

Simpson played the first nine holes with eight pars and one birdie, the birdie coming on the third hole, where he holed an eight-foot putt. That birdie took him momentarily into the lead with Stewart. If he could manage the second nine as well as the first nine, he would lead the Open easily. But he couldn't. He pitched to within a few feet for a birdie on the 11th, and led Stewart by two strokes, bogeyed the 12th by leaving a seven iron short and in the right greenside bunker, then birdied the

13th by holing a 25-foot putt.

The closing holes got him again, as they were to do so often. He missed both the 16th and 17th greens and bogeyed both holes.

So Simpson and Stewart were tied at 210, six under par, four strokes ahead of Nick Price, who had 71, and Scott Hoch, who shot 74. Price's round ended with a flourish when he birdied the 18th, the only man to do so all day.

"That felt like an eagle," Price said. "That hole is as near to a par five as you'll get."

Hoch was cruising along comfortably, looking for a steady finish until he double-bogeyed the 18th. The 18th was almost as tortuous a hole as the 16th: It gave up 30 pars, but it claimed 32 bogeys and two double bogeys.

Brian Kamm (73), Fred Couples (75), Henke (77) were at 215. At 216, even par, were Lyle, the leading European, after a 74, Irwin, Rick Fehr (73) and Craig Parry (73).

Among the high scores were Nicklaus 77; Mize, despite chipping in three times, 79; David Graham, Lanny Wadkins and Phil Mickelson, the day before his 21st birthday, 80; and Rodger Davis, 81, after shooting 68 the previous day.

Rodger Davis shot 81, 13 strokes more than in his second round.

Frustrated Craig Stadler (77-217) tossed a club to his caddie, as Ian Woosnam (79-220), oblivious, concentrated on saving his own round.

There were two golfers in the fairway and 30,000 spectators lining it. The U.S. Open had begun three days earlier with 156 competitors. Now it had come down to the last two players in the field on the last hole of the last day.

Looking at the green from the left rough was Scott Simpson, 1987 Open champion. His face was impassive, his mouth set firmly beneath its black moustache. Simpson had held the lead since the seventh hole, but now, hitting uphill and into a slight wind, he had no chance of reaching the 18th green, more than 200 yards away. He could advance the ball only 100 yards or so. A bogey five seemed likely on this 452-yard hole.

Far ahead of Simpson stood Payne Stewart having hit only his 42nd fairway of the

Payne Stewart had several chances, such as here at No. 17, for the birdie to seal a victory.

tournament, but only his ninth of the day. He was wearing the colors of the Minnesota Vikings football team and chewing hard on the wad of tobacco in his mouth. He and Simpson had begun the day tied at six under par, but now he trailed Simpson by one stroke.

In the midst of a championship, competitors such as Stewart (opposite) can seem alone in a crowd of thousands.

Stewart had 186 yards left to the hole, too far for a six iron. He chose a five iron, and, choking down on it slightly, hit it 25 feet past the hole. Then Simpson's third shot ended 25 feet from the flag, and they each began to walk up the hill to the green to receive the acclaim of the spectators.

For some holes it had been match play between them as they realized that no one was going to climb near enough to challenge them. Larry Nelson had come closest. He had been seven strokes behind at the start of the day and then birdied the fourth, sixth and seventh holes. In the 1981 Ryder Cup, Nelson was referred to by Dave Marr, the American team captain, as "my baby-faced chicken killer." He was killing chickens now, quietly and calmly, holing putt after putt.

Nelson closed to within two strokes of Stewart and three of Simpson. Playing 45 minutes ahead of Stewart and Simpson, he felt that if he could reach the clubhouse at four under par and set that as a target, they would find that hard to beat. But he couldn't quite make it. After holing a 25-foot putt for his fifth birdie of the day on

the short 13th hole, and thus moving to within three strokes of Simpson, the leader, Nelson's rally ended when he bogeyed the 14th, missing the green.

It was surprising that so few other players could challenge. The course was at its easiest, although the greens were hard and fast. "The way the course was playing today, you almost had to work at it to make a bogey," Nelson said.

He had, however, made more of a challenge than any of the others who had been close at the start of the day. Nick Price was

Scott Simpson (opposite page) struggled on the closing holes to set the stage for a playoff.

four behind overnight, but blew himself out of contention by bogeying four of his first six holes.

Scott Hoch also lay four behind, then bogeyed or double-bogeyed four of his first six holes.

Fred Couples, five behind, would end the championship three under par, but his chances had ended realistically on the eighth hole when he hit into the water.

Having fallen too far back to make a realistic challenge, Couples played steadily to finish with 70, tying for third place. "I am thrilled to finish where I did," said Couples, who was tied with Nelson, three strokes behind. "For me to play as well as

Larry Nelson drew within three strokes with his 68 and 285 total, three under par.

I did was gratifying."

The best charge of the day came from Fuzzy Zoeller, who had been nine strokes behind. "The course was there for the taking," said Zoeller, who had given his all for a five-under-par 67. This took him to two under par overall and made him one of only seven men to finish at par or better.

The Masters champion, Ian Woosnam, added an 80 for 300, a cool 12 over par. Nick Faldo had a 72 for 291, matching Sandy Lyle. The best of the vaunted Europeans was Jose Maria Olazabal, who tied for eighth place. He received as big a cheer for his fourth-round 70, which put him at 289, one over par, as Tom Watson did for his 70, which took him to 291.

Fuzzy Zoeller (opposite) placed fifth with his 67 and 286 total.

Fourth Round

Payne Stewart	72-282	-6
Scott Simpson	72-282	-6
Larry Nelson	68-285	-3
Fred Couples	70-285	-3
Fuzzy Zoeller	67-286	-2
Scott Hoch	73-287	-1
Nolan Henke	73-288	E
Raymond Floyd	68-289	+1
Jose Maria Olazabal	70-289	+1
Corey Pavin	72-289	+1
D.A. Weibring	68-290	+2
Davis Love III	71-290	+2
Jim Gallagher, Jr.	73-290	+2
Craig Parry	74-290	+2
Hale Irwin	74-290	+2

Tom Watson placed in the top 20 with a strong finish, 70 for a 291 total.

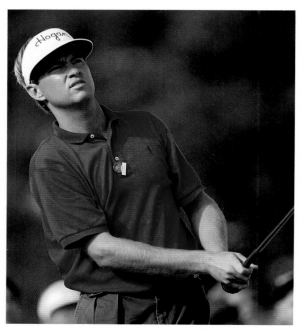

Davis Love III was under par in the first and fourth rounds.

And so it all came to the last two men, Simpson and Stewart, who, as they made their way to the 18th, had talked inconsequentially about the movie *Robin Hood* that had been on television the night before.

Stewart putted first. His ball ran five feet past. Simpson putted to within three feet.

If they both holed their second putts there would be a playoff. The pressure was on Stewart, who had to putt first and had missed makeable putts of between four and 12 feet on each of the three previous greens. He holed it. "I was pretty proud of that putt," he would say later. "That proved something to myself, that I do deserve to be playing tomorrow." It gave him his par and meant that Simpson had to hole his to force a playoff.

Simpson stepped up to the ball. The last thing he would be thinking of at this point was that he might have won the past four Opens. How? Well, he had won at Olympic in 1987. If he had played the last 18

Hale Irwin got a well-deserved reception from the spectators at the 18th hole.

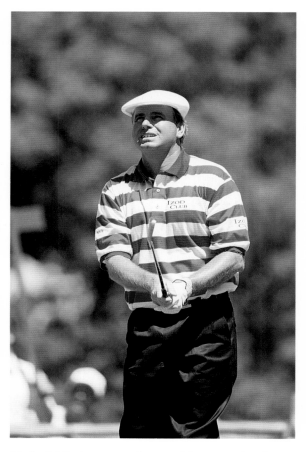

D.A. Weibring earned a top-15 exemption into the 1992 Open.

A closing 68 gave Raymond Floyd a share of eighth place.

holes in par in 1988 he would have tied Curtis Strange and Nick Faldo and joined them in a playoff. If he had played the last 18 holes in par in 1989 he would have won, stopping Strange from achieving his rare repeat victory. If he had played the last 21 holes in par in 1990 he, not Hale Irwin, would have won the Open at Medinah.

Now, though, Simpson concentrated on the tricky three-footer he needed to tie Stewart. He rapped it firmly into the hole for a bogey, the 1,715th of the Open. Stewart, who had been standing at the side of the green smiled and stepped forward to shake Simpson's hand.

They had each shot 72 to finish the championship at 282, six under par, three ahead of their nearest challengers and one more than Tony Jacklin's winning total 21 years

previously. Thus, the 91st U.S. Open would be decided by an 18-hole playoff, the third in four years and the 30th in all. Not everyone was thrilled.

"For the fans' sakes I think they should see the champion crowned today," said Stewart, an opinion he was to reiterate a day later. "A four- or five-hole playoff seems a good idea to me," said Simpson.

"We discuss playoff changes every year, but we feel this event is important enough that we want to stay with an 18-hole playoff," said David Fay, executive director of the USGA. "There is no serious consideration given to changing the format. We feel that an 18-hole round of golf is the unit of measurement for stroke play. This is our national championship. We feel this is the proper way to do it."

91st U.S. Open

The Playoff

There were two golfers in the fairway and 30,000 spectators lining it. Just a minute, that's what happened Sunday. This is Monday.

But the end of Monday's playoff between Scott Simpson and Payne Stewart was uncannily like the end of Sunday's fourth round. The same two men came to the last few holes with nothing to choose between them. It had been a scrappy afternoon's golf—11 bogeys between them so far— but at least it hadn't been as one-sided as it had at Winged Foot in 1984 when Fuzzy Zoeller won by eight strokes over Greg Norman, or at The Country Club in 1988 when Curtis Strange defeated Nick Faldo by four strokes. One stroke separated Simpson and Stewart on the 18th tee, the 90th hole, just as it had on the same tee and the 72nd hole 24 hours earlier. One difference: This time Stewart led by one stroke.

They had teed off precisely at 12:30 p.m.

The champion at last, Payne Stewart (opposite) celebrated his U.S. Open title.

Scott Simpson couldn't believe it at No. 16 when he missed a three-foot putt for a bogey, enabling Stewart to tie him with a birdie from 18 feet.

on a hot, clear day. Stewart quickly took the lead. He chipped close on the first hole while standing with one shoe in a bunker and the other outside it; he used the toe of his putter to roll his ball to within inches of the hole on the second. Simpson, meanwhile, was bunkered on the first and didn't get up and down, and he three-putted the second green.

The fifth hole was the first of three holes on which there was a two-stroke swing. Simpson's second, a stunning six iron, eased within three feet of the flag for an easy birdie. Stewart's ball flew left of a bunker on the left of the green, landing in thick rough from where he tried to flop the ball out as if it were in sand. It flopped out all right— into the bunker in front of him, and he did well to get up and down from there for a bogey five.

The seventh is a tantalizing par five, its fairway sweeping in an easy curve around a bend, then running gently downhill to a green set at an angle to the fairway. There are bunkers beyond it and water in front of it. At 518 yards, it is the shortest par five on the course and clearly reachable in two

51

but only if the drive remains in the fairway. Stewart's drive didn't. It bounded into the right rough and from there he could only pitch out, pitch on to the green and two-putt for a par.

Simpson's drive, though, went 15 yards farther and straighter, putting him in position to go for the green with his second. He hit a three iron that rolled off the green, but stopped pin high and 15 feet to the right of the flag. He chipped to four feet and one-putted for his second birdie in three holes. Also, he took the lead for the first time.

Simpson might have gone further ahead on the eighth but for an outrageous piece of luck that befell Stewart. Stewart's tee shot landed in the water to the right of the green but rebounded off a rock beneath the surface into the rough at the edge of the pond. Stewart took three more strokes to get

down, but the rock had most likely saved him one stroke.

Simpson is not a demonstrative man, and after skilfully fading his shot back in towards the flag only to see it trickle over the green, he gave a rare display of emotion. He let his club fall to the ground. He dropped it again when his first putt slid past the hole. It was an uncanny break for Stewart, and later he admitted that after it had happened he began to think it was his day.

They reached the turn in two hours and five minutes, hardly the speed of light, with Simpson one stroke ahead. He had gone out in 37, Stewart in 38.

On the 10th hole, Simpson missed a four-footer and thus recorded his fifth bogey of the day. Stewart parred and now the two of them were level once again. This was

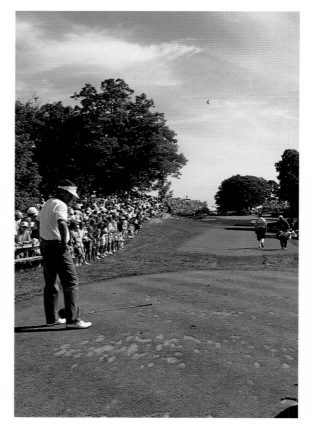

Stewart (left) hit a superb five iron at No. 17 to within 20 feet of the hole. It was then Simpson's turn, and Simpson (right) was disconsolate after his four iron hit the bank of a pond and jumped into the water. Simpson salvaged a bogey, but stood one stroke down with one hole to play.

how they remained until the short 13th, which Simpson three-putted from 30 feet, falling behind for the first time since the fifth hole. It was his second three-putt green of the day.

It was Stewart's turn to make mistakes on the 14th and 15th holes, and allow Simpson to edge ahead by two strokes. Stewart's approach to the 14th green stopped short of the green, and with a bunker eating into his intended line, he had to work hard to pitch over the bunker and two-putt. Then he three-putted the 15th from 60 feet.

Now Simpson led by two strokes with three holes to play, just as he had on Sunday afternoon.

"Even when I was two down after 15, I didn't quit," Stewart said later. "A lot can happen on the way to the clubhouse."

The 16th had been the pivotal hole all week. Stewart had always parred it— so far. This time he rammed in an 18-foot putt for a birdie (his first of the day) that so rattled Simpson he missed his three-foot second putt for his third three-putt of the round. Another two-stroke swing, the third of the round, and now they were even with two holes to play.

The difference this made to the two men was evident on the 17th tee. Stewart hit a glorious five iron 20 feet past the hole. Simpson's four iron started left, hit a bank, and jumped into a pond by the side of the green. His reaction told it all. He dropped his club, crossed his arms and looked disconsolate. Still, Simpson made an excellent recovery by taking a penalty drop nearby, pitched to within 10 feet, and holed the putt for a bogey four.

Stewart's second putt was very important. It was four feet with a little left-to-right break on it, and he talked to himself as he lined it up from all angles. "This is it, buddy," he thought as he prowled around

Spectators, young and old, viewed the action.

the hole. "For you to be champion you've got to make this putt. You've practiced it often enough. Now do it." He did. Now he led by one stroke with one hole to play.

Stewart used his one iron from the 18th tee, and his ball ran into a bunker on the right of the fairway. He had a good lie in the middle of the bunker, and with a six iron hit his ball to the right front of the green, 50 feet from the flag.

Simpson's ball landed in the same bunker as Stewart's, but scooted through and into rough beyond. This was a lucky break. He almost certainly wouldn't have been able to hit his ball high enough to clear the high front wall of the bunker and far enough to reach the green. Instead, he hit an iron 215 yards to the back right fringe of the green. He knew he had to hole his chip to stand a chance of tying Stewart. He had played delicate chips like this on at least four other greens in the round. Nevertheless, he could get no closer than 10 feet beyond the hole. Then he missed the putt. It was his third successive bogey and his eighth of the day. He shot 77.

It left Stewart with two putts from four feet to win. As Simpson's caddie draped a consoling arm around his employer, they stood side by side and watched Stewart putt for victory. He holed it.

Stewart's three-over-par 75 was the highest winning score in a U.S. Open playoff since Tommy Armour shot 76 to Harry Cooper's 79 in 1927, and he was the first champion since Jack Nicklaus at Baltusrol in 1980 to lead from the start.

As Stewart and Simpson were escorted back to the green they had left only moments ago, the public address system crackled into life. It was Grant Spaeth, president of the USGA. His opening words were, "Thank you, Minnesota." They were very appropriate.

91st
U.S. Open
The Champion

Payne Stewart, the 91st U.S. Open champion, may wear violet-colored clothes but he is no shrinking violet.

In Britain, he is remembered as the man who appeared to be wrapped in a massive American flag in the fourth round of the 1990 British Open at St. Andrews. Stewart, wrote one journalist, "looked as though he was dressed for burial at sea."

Without fail, Stewart dons knickers in tournaments, and the toes and heels of his $500 white golf shoes are tipped with brass. For a while, he wore acupuncture needles in his earlobes to calm his temper and his nerves. As if that was not enough to make him somewhat different from your run-of-the-mill touring pro, he also plays the harmonica in the band called Jake Trout and the Flounders, a band led by Peter Jacobsen, with sidemen.

After his Open victory, Stewart deserves to be remembered less as golf's peacock, a worthy descendent in matters sartorial of Jimmy Demaret and Doug Sanders, and more as one of the world's best golfers. His victory in the Open was his second in the past seven major championships. Only one other current player in the world could match that—Nick Faldo, of England.

The ultimate test of a golfer is his performance in the major championships and how he plays the closing holes of these events. These are the moments when the stomach starts churning and the palms begin to sweat. For Scott Simpson, Stewart's opponent, the challenge of the 16th, 17th and 18th holes at Hazeltine National Golf Club, which are among the fiercest of any course

The new U.S. Open champion was dressed for the part.

currently staging major championships, was too much. For these three holes, Simpson was eight over par for five rounds. Stewart was one under par.

Furthermore, Stewart played a series of stunning shots that were unforgettable to anyone fortunate enough to see them. A long putt on the 16th green on Sunday afternoon, an eight iron that flew over a 50-foot-high ash tree and was followed by an 18-foot putt that bolted into the cup on the 16th hole of the playoff, and a five iron that never wavered from its target on the 17th hole were four of the best. Perhaps the best of all was the six iron he played from a bunker on the 18th in the playoff, a shot that could have been ruined had he taken as little as a teaspoonful of sand.

With strokes such as these, Stewart nailed a lie that had been circulating— that he hadn't the heart to win when heart, not skill, is the most important requirement. The lie was well-founded because time and again Stewart had played himself into a challenging position only to falter. As long ago as 1987, Lee Trevino said, "Stewart has no weaknesses. He is the next great player."

But he did have one weakness. He couldn't finish things off. He could edge close enough to victory to smell it, but never close enough to taste it. Between 1984 and 1989 he finished second 12 times and had 58 top-10 finishes, but only three victories. "Payne didn't seem to know how to finish tournaments," Jack Nicklaus said at the time. "He always seemed to make the crucial mistake. He squandered a lot of opportunities." His playoff record before the Open was one for six.

Even when Stewart birdied four of the

55

last five holes and won the 1989 PGA Championship, his first major title, it was said that he only won because Mike Reid collapsed, dropping three strokes on the 16th and 17th holes. Later that year, Stewart lost the last two holes against Jose Maria Olazabal in the Ryder Cup singles, losing his match by one hole, and then lost the Nabisco Championship to Tom Kite by three-putting the 72nd green and three-putting the second hole of a playoff. Indeed, his playoff record leading up to the Open left something to be desired.

So there was some feeling in one comment he made after beating Simpson: "A lot of people said I backed into that one (the PGA). I didn't back into this one."

Stewart, the possessor of a lovely rhythmical swing with the most beautiful turn in golf, according to Ben Crenshaw, should go on and win more tournaments. He is at the peak of his career and the leading current American player. Of those American golfers who are younger than Tom Watson, only three have won

Chelsea Stewart, age 5, was proud of her dad.

multiple majors, Fuzzy Zoeller, Curtis Strange and now Stewart. He is 34 years old, and has done his apprenticeship, albeit that it seemed to take him a longer time than some. Players like Crenshaw and Lanny Wadkins were top amateurs, and for them the learning process began when they won amateur events. By the time they turned pro, they started winning quickly. Stewart took longer, but on Monday he finally demonstrated he has learned the knack now.

"Payne has a great swing. He hits a lot of good irons and he putts really well," Simpson said after the playoff. "He doesn't miss many six- to eight-footers. At least he didn't these past few days. On the 11th, for instance, after I missed my birdie putt from 15 feet, I just knew he would hole his from 10 feet for a five. I just knew he would, and he did."

"What do I do well?" Stewart asked rhetorically in answer to a question. "I have great imagination for hitting golf shots. I am a very good iron player and, believe it or not, I'm a pretty good putter."

Stewart's physical fitness, however, unlike his golf, needs a lot of attention. He overcomes a lower back injury by doing stretching exercises morning and evening and wearing what looks like a black scuba suit under his golf clothes. The upper neck injury he suffered at the beginning of this year, which forced him to spend 10 weeks at home wearing a neck brace and left him so weak in his left arm he couldn't lift a two-pound weight, may have been a blessing in disguise.

Until then, Stewart had a name for being arrogant. Ken Green, a colleague, has said he thought Stewart was spoiled and snobby, which, coming from Green, sounds like the pot calling the kettle black. Stewart said on Monday his neck injury had made him realize he was human and that there were more important things in life than golf, for example his wife, Tracey, and children, Chelsea and Aaron.

He spoke as if he had discovered the secret to the perennial problem that touring pros face, the feeling that Curtis Strange had talked about as well, "When I'm at home I wish I was out on Tour and when I'm out on Tour I wish I was back with my family."

"I think you need arrogance on the golf course, a self-belief," said Stewart. "Arrogance off the course won't help you win friends and influence people."

As Stewart spoke, he was wearing a football ensemble—Super Bowl XXVI in honor of next January's staging of the Super Bowl in Minneapolis' Metrodome. He has a contract with the National Football League to wear the colors of its member teams. His taste for peacock colors came from his late father, a salesman who wore check jackets and check trousers in order to stand out from other salesmen. In 1982, wearing a white shirt, red trousers and white shoes, Stewart found himself hitting shots on a practice tee next to another pro identically dressed. His father's words came back to him, and at that moment he decided to start wearing knickers. He hasn't looked back since.

Stewart cried in victory, another trait he inherited from his father. Then, before flying home to Florida en route to the Irish Open in Killarney, he ordered champagne to be served to journalists waiting to interview him. Champagne Payne doesn't have a bad ring to it. And Champion Payne doesn't sound bad, either.

Autograph time for visors, programs—and just-developed photos.

91st
U.S. Open
Statistics

Hole	1	2	3	4	5	6	7	8	9	10	11	12	13	14	15	16	17	18	Total
Par	4	4	5	3	4	4	5	3	4	4	5	4	3	4	5	4	3	4	72

Payne Stewart

	1	2	3	4	5	6	7	8	9	10	11	12	13	14	15	16	17	18		
Round 1	3	4	4	2	4	4	5	3	4	4	4	4	3	4	4	4	3	4	67	
Round 2	4	3	5	3	3	4	4	4	4	4	5	4	3	4	5	4	3	4	70	
Round 3	4	4	4	3	6	4	5	3	4	4	4	4	4	4	5	4	3	4	73	
Round 4	4	4	4	3	4	5	5	3	4	4	5	4	3	4	5	4	3	4	72	282
Playoff	4	4	5	3	5	4	5	4	4	4	5	4	3	5	6	3	3	4	75	

Scott Simpson

	1	2	3	4	5	6	7	8	9	10	11	12	13	14	15	16	17	18		
Round 1	5	4	5	3	4	4	4	2	4	4	5	4	3	3	5	5	3	3	70	
Round 2	3	4	5	3	3	5	4	2	4	4	4	4	3	4	4	4	4	4	68	
Round 3	4	4	4	3	4	4	5	3	4	4	4	5	2	4	5	5	4	4	72	
Round 4	4	4	5	3	4	4	4	3	4	3	5	4	3	4	5	5	3	5	72	282
Playoff	5	5	5	3	3	4	4	4	4	5	5	4	4	3	5	5	4	5	77	

Hole	Par	Eagles	Birdies	Pars	Bogeys	Higher	Rank	Average
1	4	1	34	272	118	14	5	4.252
2	4	0	57	305	71	6	14	4.061
3	5	0	72	282	80	5	16	5.041
4	3	2	47	297	89	4	12	3.107
5	4	0	56	258	111	14	9	4.191
6	4	0	36	280	114	9	7	4.223
7	5	3	155	223	55	3	18	4.774
8	3	0	51	282	71	35	8	3.218
9	4	0	37	281	106	15	6	4.227
OUT	36	6	545	2480	815	105		37.094
10	4	0	66	287	72	14	13	4.079
11	5	1	96	269	64	9	17	4.965
12	4	1	33	271	120	14	4	4.259
13	3	0	28	274	124	13	3	3.280
14	4	0	59	265	104	11	11	4.154
15	5	0	72	282	78	7	15	5.047
16	4	0	41	249	103	46	1	4.398
17	3	0	45	290	86	18	10	3.182
18	4	0	25	255	149	10	2	4.328
IN	36	2	465	2442	900	142		37.692
TOTAL	72	8	1010	4922	1715	247		74.786

Date	Winner, Runner-Up	Score	Site	Entry
1895 (Oct.)	**Horace Rawlins**	173	**Newport G.C.,**	11
	Willie Dunn	175	Newport R.I.	
1896 (July)	**James Foulis**	†152	**Shinnecock Hills G.C.,**	35
	Horace Rawlins	155	Southampton, N.Y.	
1897 (Sept.)	**Joe Lloyd**	162	**Chicago, G.C.,**	35
	Willie Anderson	163	Wheaton, Ill.	
1898 (June)	**Fred Herd**	328	**Myopia Hunt Club,**	49
	Alex Smith	335	S. Hamilton, Mass.	
1899 (Sept.)	**Willie Smith**	315	**Baltimore C.C.,**	81
	George Low/Val Fitzjohn/W.H. Way	326	(Roland Park Course) Baltimore, Md.	
1900 (Oct.)	**Harry Vardon**	313	**Chicago G.C.,**	60
	J.H. Taylor	315	Wheaton, Ill.	
1901 (June)	**Willie Anderson**	331-85	**Myopia Hunt Club,**	60
	Alex Smith	331-86	S. Hamilton, Mass.	
1902 (Oct.)	**Lawrence Auchterlonie**	307	**Garden City, G.C.,**	90
	Stewart Gardner/*Walter J. Travis	313	Garden City, N.Y.	
1903 (June)	**Willie Anderson**	307-82	**Baltusrol G.C.,**	89
	David Brown	307-84	(original course) Springfield, N.J.	
1904 (July)	**Willie Anderson**	303	**Glen View Club,**	71
	Gilbert Nicholls	308	Golf, Ill.	
1905 (Sept.)	**Willie Anderson**	314	**Myopia Hunt Club,**	83
	Alex Smith	316	S. Hamilton, Mass.	
1906 (June)	**Alex Smith**	295	**Onwentsia Club,**	68
	William Smith	302	Lake Forest, Ill.	
1907 (June)	**Alex Ross**	302	**Philadelphia Cricket C.,**	82
	Gilbert Nicholls	304	(St. Martins Course) Philadelphia, Pa.	
1908 (Aug.)	**Fred McLeod**	322-77	**Myopia Hunt Club,**	88
	Willie Smith	322-83	S. Hamilton, Mass.	
1909 (June)	**George Sargent**	290	**Englewood G.C.,**	84
	Tom McNamara	294	Englewood, N.Y.	
1910 (June)	**Alex Smith**	298-71	**Philadelphia Cricket C.,**	75
	John J. McDermott	298-75	(St. Martins Course) Philadelphia, Pa.	
	Macdonald Smith	298-77		
1911 (June)	**John J. McDermott**	307-80	**Chicago G.C.,**	79
	Michael J. Brady	307-82	Wheaton, Ill.	
	George O. Simpson	307-85		
1912 (Aug.)	**John J. McDermott**	294	**C.C. of Buffalo,**	131
	Tom McNamara	296	Buffalo, N.Y.	
1913 (Sept.)	***Francis Ouimet**	304-72	**The Country Club,**	165
	Harry Vardon	304-77	Brookline, Mass.	
	Edward Ray	304-78		
1914 (Aug.)	**Walter Hagen**	290	**Midlothian C.C.,**	129
	*Charles Evans, Jr.	291	Blue Island, Ill.	
1915 (June)	***Jerone D. Travers**	297	**Baltusrol G.C.,**	141
	Tom McNamara	298	(original course,) Springfield, N.J.	
1916 (June)	***Charles Evans, Jr.**	286	**Minikahda Club,**	94
	Jock Hutchinson	288	Minneapolis, Minn.	
1917-18 — No Championships: World War I				
1919 (June)	**Walter Hagen**	301-77	**Brae Burn C.C.,**	142
	Michael J. Brady	301-78	West Newton, Mass.	
1920 (Aug.)	**Edward Ray**	295	**Inverness Club,**	265
	Harry Vardon/Jack Burke, Sr./	296	Toledo, Ohio	
	Leo Diegel/Jock Hutchison			
1921 (July)	**James M. Barnes**	289	**Columbia C.C.,**	262
	Walter Hagen/Fred McLeod	298	Chevy Chase, Md.	
1922 (July)	**Gene Sarazen**	288	**Skokie C.C.,**	323
	*Robert T. Jones, Jr./John L. Black	289	Glencoe, Ill.	
1923 (July)	***Robert T. Jones, Jr.**	296-76	**Inwood C.C.,**	360
	Bobby Cruickshank	296-78	Inwood, N.Y.	

Date	Winner, Runner-Up	Score	Site	Entry
1924 (June)	**Cyril Walker** *Robert T. Jones, Jr.	297 300	**Oakland Hills C.C.,** (South Course) Birmingham, Mich.	319
1925 (June)	**William Macfarlane** *Robert T. Jones, Jr.	291-75-72 291-75-73	**Worcester C.C.,** Worcester, Mass.	445
1926 (June)	***Robert T. Jones, Jr.** Joe Turnesa	293 294	**Scioto C.C.,** Columbus, Ohio	694
1927 (June)	**Tommy Armour** Harry Cooper	301-76 301-79	**Oakmont C.C.,** Oakmont, Pa.	898
1928 (June)	**Johnny Farrell** *Robert T. Jones, Jr.	294-143 294-144	**Olympia Fields C.C.,** (No. 4 Course) Mateson, Ill.	1,064
1929 (June)	***Robert T. Jones, Jr.** Al Espinosa	294-141 294-164	**Winged Foot G.C.,** (West Course) Mamaroneck, N.Y.	1,000
1930 (July)	***Robert T. Jones, Jr.** Macdonald Smith	287 289	**Interlachen C.C.,** Minneapolis, Minn.	1,177
1931 (July)	**Billy Burke** George Von Elm	292-149-148 292-149-149	**Inverness Club,** Toledo, Ohio	1,141
1932 (June)	**Gene Sarazen** Bobby Cruickshank/T. Philip Perkins	286 289	**Fresh Meadow C.C.,** Flushing, N.Y.	1,011
1933 (June)	***John Goodman** Ralph Guldahl	287 288	**North Shore, C.C.,** Glenview, Ill.	915
1934 (June)	**Olin Dutra** Gene Sarazen	293 294	**Merion Cricket C.,** (East Course) Ardmore, Pa.	1,063
1935 (June)	**Sam Parks, Jr.** Jimmy Thomson	299 301	**Oakmont C.C.,** Oakmont, Pa.	1,125
1936 (June)	**Tony Manero** Harry Cooper	282 284	**Baltusrol G.C.,** (Upper Course) Springfield, N.Y.	1,277
1937 (June)	**Ralph Guldahl** Sam Snead	281 283	**Oakland Hills C.C.,** (South Course) Birmingham, Mich.	1,402
1938 (June)	**Ralph Guldahl** Dick Metz	284 290	**Cherry Hills C.C.,** Englewood, Colo.	1,223
1939 (June)	**Byron Nelson** Craig Wood Denny Shute	284-68-70 284-68-73 284-76	**Philadelphia C.C.,** (Spring Mill Course) West Conshohocken, Pa.	1,193
1940 (June)	**Lawson Little** Gene Sarazen	287-70 287-73	**Canterbury, G.C.,** Cleveland, Ohio	1,161
1941 (June)	**Craig Wood** Denny Shute	284 287	**Colonial Club,** Fort Worth, Tex.	1,048
1942-45 — No Championships: World War II				
1946 (June)	**Lloyd Mangrum** Byron Nelson/Victor Ghezzi	284-72-72 284-72-73	**Canterbury, G.C.,** Cleveland, Ohio	1,175
1947 (June)	**Lew Worsham** Sam Snead	282-69 282-70	**St. Louis G.C.,** Clayton, Mo.	1,356
1948 (June)	**Ben Hogan** Jimmy Demaret	276 278	**Riviera C.C.,** Los Angeles, Calif.	1,411
1949 (June)	**Cary Middlecoff** Sam Snead/Clayton Heafner	286 287	**Medinah C.C.,** (No. 3 Course) Medinah, Ill.	1,348
1950 (June)	**Ben Hogan** Lloyd Mangrum George Fazio	287-69 287-73 287-75	**Merion G.C.,** (East Course) Ardmore, Pa.	1,379
1951 (June)	**Ben Hogan** Clayton Heafner	287 289	**Oakland Hills C.C.,** (South Course) Birmingham, Mich.	1,511
1952 (June)	**Julius Boros** Ed (Porky) Oliver	281 285	**Northwood Club,** Dallas, Tex.	1,688
1953 (June)	**Ben Hogan** Sam Snead	283 289	**Oakmont C.C.,** Oakmont, Pa.	1,669
1954 (June)	**Ed Furgol** Gene Littler	284 285	**Baltusrol G.C.,** (Lower Course) Springfield, N. J.	1,928
1955 (June)	**Jack Fleck** Ben Hogan	287-69 287-72	**Olympic Club,** (Lake Course) San Francisco, Calif.	1,522
1956 (June)	**Cary Middlecoff** Julius Boros/Ben Hogan	281 282	**Oak Hill C.C.,** (East Course) Rochester, N.Y.	1,921
1957 (June)	**Dick Mayer** Cary Middlecoff	282-72 282-79	**Inverness Club,** Toledo, Ohio	1,907
1958 (June)	**Tommy Bolt** Gary Player	283 287	**Southern Hills C.C.,** Tulsa, Okla.	2,132
1959 (June)	**Bill Casper, Jr.** Bob Rosburg	282 283	**Winged Foot G.C.,** (West Course) Mamaroneck, N.Y.	2,385

Date	Winners, Runner-Up	Score	Site	Entry
1960 (June)	**Arnold Palmer** *Jack Nicklaus	280 282	**Cherry Hills C.C.,** Englewood, Colo.	2,453
1961 (June)	**Gene Littler** Doug Sanders/Bob Goalby	281 282	**Oakland Hills C.C.,** (South Course) Birmingham, Mich.	2,449
1962 (June)	**Jack Nicklaus** Arnold Palmer	283-71 283-74	**Oakmont, C.C.,** Oakmont, Pa.	2,475
1963 (June)	**Julius Boros** Jacky Cupit Arnold Palmer	293-70 293-73 293-76	**The Country Club** Brookline, Mass.	2,392
1964 (June)	**Ken Venturi** Tommy Jacobs	278 282	**Congressional C.C.,** Washington, D.C.	2,341
1965 (June)	**Gary Player** Kel Nagel	282-71 282-74	**Bellerive C.C.,** St. Louis, Mo.	2,271
1966 (June)	**Bill Casper, Jr.** Arnold Palmer	278-69 278-73	**Olympic Club,** (Lake Course) San Francisco, Calif.	2,475
1967 (June)	**Jack Nicklaus** Arnold Palmer	275 279	**Baltusrol G.C.,** (Lower Course) Springfield, N.J.	2,651
1968 (June)	**Lee Trevino** Jack Nicklaus	275 279	**Oak Hill C.C.,** (East Course) Rochester, N.Y.	3,007
1969 (June)	**Orville Moody** Deane Beman/Al Geiberger/Bob Rosburg	281 282	**Champions G.C.,** (Cypress Creek Course) Houston, Tex.	3,397
1970 (June)	**Tony Jacklin** Dave Hill	281 288	**Hazeltine National G.C.,** Chaska, Minn.	3,605
1971 (June)	**Lee Trevino** Jack Nicklaus	280-68 280-71	**Merion G.C.,** (East Course) Ardmore, Pa.	4,279
1972 (June)	**Jack Nicklaus** Bruce Crampton	290 293	**Pebble Beach G.L.,** Pebble Beach, Calif.	4,196
1973 (June)	**John Miller** John Schlee	279 280	**Oakmont C.C.,** Oakmont, Pa.	3,580
1974 (June)	**Hale Irwin** Forrest Fezler	287 289	**Winged Foot G.C.,** (West Course) Mamaroneck, N.Y.	3,914
1975 (June)	**Lou Graham** John Mahaffey	287-71 287-73	**Medinah C.C.,** (No. 3 Course) Medinah, Ill.	4,214
1976 (June)	**Jerry Pate** Tom Weiskopf/Al Geiberger	277 279	**Atlanta Athletic C.,** Duluth, Ga.	4,436
1977 (June)	**Hubert Green** Lou Graham	278 279	**Southern Hills C.C.,** Tulsa, Okla.	4,608
1978 (June)	**Andy North** J.C. Snead/Dave Stockton	285 286	**Cherry Hills C.C.,** Englewood, Colo.	4,897
1979 (June)	**Hale Irwin** Gary Player/Jerry Pate	284 286	**Inverness Club,** Toledo, Ohio	4,853
1980 (June)	**Jack Nicklaus** Isao Aoki	†272 274	**Baltusrol G.C.,** (Lower Course) Springfield, N. J.	4,812
1981 (June)	**David Graham** Bill Rogers/George Burns	273 276	**Merion G.C.,** (East Course) Ardmore, Pa.	4,946
1982 (June)	**Tom Watson** Jack Nicklaus	282 284	**Pebble Beach G.L.,** Pebble Beach, Calif.	5,255
1983 (June)	**Larry Nelson** Tom Watson	280 281	**Oakmont C.C.,** Oakmont, Pa.	5,039
1984 (June)	**Fuzzy Zoeller** Greg Norman	276-67 276-75	**Winged Foot G.C.,** (West Course) Mamaroneck, N.Y.	5,195
1985 (June)	**Andy North** Chen Tze-Chung/Denis Watson/Dave Barr	279 280	**Oakland Hills C.C.,** (South Course) Birmingham, Mich.	5,274
1986 (June)	**Raymond Floyd** Lanny Wadkins/Chip Beck	279 281	**Shinnecock Hills G.C.,** Southampton, N.Y.	5,410
1987 (June)	**Scott Simpson** Tom Watson	277 278	**Olympic Club,** (Lake Course) San Francisco, Calif.	5,696
1988 (June)	**Curtis Strange** Nick Faldo	278-71 278-75	**The Country Club,** Brookline, Mass.	5,775
1989 (June)	**Curtis Strange** Chip Beck/Mark McCumber/Ian Woosnam	278 279	**Oak Hill C.C.,** (East Course) Rochester, N.Y.	5,786
1990 (June)	**Hale Irwin** Mike Donald	280-74/3 280-74/4	**Medinah C.C.** (No. 3 Course) Medinah, Ill.	§6,198
1991 (June)	**Payne Stewart** Scott Simpson	282-75 282-77	**Hazeltine National G.C.** Chaska, Minn.	6,063

†Record Score   *Denotes Amateur   § Record Entry

Oldest champion (years/months/days)
45/0/15 — Hale Irwin (1990)

Youngest champion
19/10/14 — John J. McDermott (1911)

Most victories
4 — Willie Anderson (1901, 03, 04, 05)
4 — Robert T. Jones, Jr. (1923, 26, 29, 30)
4 — Ben Hogan (1948, 50, 51, 53)
4 — Jack Nicklaus (1962, 67, 72, 80)
3 — Hale Irwin (1974, 79, 90)
2 — by 11 players: Alex Smith (1906, 10),
John J. McDermott (1911, 12), Walter
Hagen (1914, 19), Gene Sarazen (1922, 32),
Ralph Guldhal (1937, 38), Cary Middlecoff
(1949, 56), Julius Boros (1952, 63), Bill
Casper (1959, 66), Lee Trevino (1968, 71),
Andy North (1978, 85), and Curtis
Strange (1988, 89).

Consecutive victories
Willie Anderson (1903, 04, 05)
John J. McDermott (1911, 12)
Robert T. Jones, Jr. (1929, 30)
Ralph Guldhal (1937, 38)
Ben Hogan (1950, 51)
Curtis Strange (1988, 89)

Most times runner-up
4 — Sam Snead
4 — Robert T. Jones, Jr.
4 — Arnold Palmer
4 — Jack Nicklaus

Longest course
7,195 yards — Medinah C.C. (No. 3 Course),
Medinah, Ill. (1990)

Shortest course
Since World War II
6,528 yards — Merion G.C. (East Course),
Ardmore, Pa. (1971, 81)

Most often host club of Open
6 — Baltusrol G.C., Springfield, N.J. (1903, 15,
36, 54, 67, 80)
6 — Oakmont (Pa.) C.C. (1927, 35, 53, 62, 73,
83)

Largest entry
6,198 (1990)

Smallest entry
11 (1895)

Lowest score, 72 holes
272 — Jack Nicklaus (63-71-70-68), at Baltusrol
G.C. (Lower Course), Springfield, N.J.
(1980)

Lowest score, first 54 holes
203 — George Burns (69-66-68), at Merion
G.C. (East Course), Ardmore, Pa. (1981)

203 — Tze-Chung Chen (65-69-69), at Oakland
Hills C.C. (South Course), Birmingham,
Mich. (1985)

Lowest score, last 54 holes
204 — Jack Nicklaus (67-72-65), at Baltusrol
G.C. (Lower Course), Springfield, N.J.
(1967)
204 — Raymond Floyd (68-70-66), at
Shinnecock Hills G.C., Southampton, N.Y.
(1986)

Lowest score, first 36 holes
134 — Jack Nicklaus (63-71), at Baltusrol G.C.
(Lower Course), Springfield, N.J. (1980)
134 — Tze-Chung Chen (65-69), at Oakland
Hills C.C. (South Course), Birmingham,
Mich. (1985)

Lowest score, last 36 holes
132 — Larry Nelson (65-67), at Oakmont C.C.,
Oakmont, Pa. (1983)

Lowest score, 9 holes
30 — on 14 occasions, most recently by Scott
Simpson (first nine, second round), Paul
Azinger (first nine, fourth round), and
Peter Jacobsen (first nine, fourth round) at
The Country Club, Brookline, Mass.
(1988)

Lowest score, 18 holes
63 — Johnny Miller, fourth round at Oakmont
(Pa.) C.C. (1973)
63 — Jack Nicklaus, first round at Baltusrol
G.C. (Lower Course), Springfield, N.J.
(1980)
63 — Tom Weiskopf, first round at Baltusrol
G.C. (Lower Course), Springfield, N.J.
(1980)

Largest winning margin
11 — Willie Smith (315), at Baltimore (Md.)
C.C. (Roland Park Course) (1899)

Highest winning score
Since World War II
293 — Julius Boros, at The Country Club,
Brookline, Mass. (1963) (won in playoff)

Best start by champion
63 — Jack Nicklaus, at Baltusrol G.C. (Lower
Course), Springfield, N.J. (1980)

Best finish by champion
63 — Johnny Miller, at Oakmont (Pa.) C.C.
(1973)

Worst start by champion
Since World War II
76 — Ben Hogan, at Oakland Hills C.C.
(South Course), Birmingham, Mich. (1951)
76 — Jack Fleck, at The Olympic Club (Lake

Course), San Francisco, Calif. (1955)

Worst finish by champion

Since World War II

75 — Cary Middlecoff, at Medinah C.C.
(No. 3 Course), Medinah, Ill. (1949)

75 — Hale Irwin, at Inverness Club, Toledo,
Ohio (1979)

Lowest score to lead field, 18 holes

63 — Jack Nicklaus and Tom Weiskopf, at
Baltusrol G.C. (Lower Course), Springfield, N.J. (1980)

Lowest score to lead field, 36 holes

134 — Jack Nicklaus (63-71), at Baltusrol G.C.
(Lower Course), Springfield, N.J. (1980)

134 — Tze-Chung Chen (65-69), at Oakland
Hills C.C. (South Course), Birmingham,
Mich. (1985)

Lowest score to lead field, 54 holes

203 — George Burns (69-66-68), at Merion
G.C. (East Course), Ardmore, Pa. (1981)

203 — Tze-Chung Chen (65-69-69), at Oakland
Hills C.C. (South Course), Birmingham,
Mich. (1985)

Highest score to lead field, 18 holes

Since World War II

71 — Sam Snead, at Oakland Hills C.C.
(South Course), Birmingham, Mich. (1951)

71 — Tommy Bolt, Julius Boros, and Dick
Metz, at Southern Hills C.C., Tulsa, Okla.
(1958)

71 — Tony Jacklin, at Hazeltine National
G.C., Chaska, Minn. (1970)

71 — Orville Moody, Jack Nicklaus, Chi Chi
Rodriguez, Mason Rudolph, Tom Shaw,
and Kermit Zarley, at Pebble Beach
(Calif.) Golf Links (1972)

Highest score to lead field, 36 holes

Since World War II

144 — Bobby Locke (73-71), at Oakland Hills
C.C. (South Course), Birmingham, Mich.
(1951)

144 — Tommy Bolt (67-77) and E. Harvie
Ward (74-70), at The Olympic Club (Lake
Course), San Francisco, Calif. (1955)

144 — Homero Blancas (74-70), Bruce
Crampton (74-70), Jack Nicklaus (71-73),
Cesar Seduno (72-72), Lanny Wadkins
(76-68) and Kermit Zarley (71-73), at
Pebble Beach (Calif.) Golf Links (1972)

Highest score to lead field, 54 holes

Since World War II

218 — Bobby Locke (73-71-74), at Oakland
Hills C.C. (South Course), Birmingham,
Mich. (1951)

218 — Jacky Cupit (70-72-76), at The Country
Club, Brookline, Mass. (1963)

Highest 36-hole cut

155 — at The Olympic Club (Lakeside
Course), San Francisco, Calif. (1955)

Most players to tie for lead, 18 holes

7 — at Pebble Beach (Calif.) Golf Links (1972);
at Southern Hills C.C., Tulsa, Okla.
(1977); and at Shinnecock Hills G.C.,
Southampton, N.Y. (1896)

Most players to tie for lead, 36 holes

6 — at Pebble Beach (Calif.) Golf Links (1972)

Most players to tie for lead, 54 holes

4 — at Oakmont (Pa.) C.C. (1973)

Most sub-par rounds, championship

124 — at Medinah C.C. (No. 3 Course),
Medinah, Ill. (1990)

Most sub-par 72-hole totals, championship

28 — at Medinah C.C. (No. 3 Course),
Medinah, Ill. (1990)

Most sub-par scores, first round

39 — at Medinah C.C. (No. 3 Course),
Medinah, Ill. (1990)

Most sub-par scores, second round

47 — at Medinah C.C. (No. 3 Course),
Medinah, Ill. (1990)

Most sub-par scores, third round

24 — at Medinah C.C. (No. 3 Course),
Medinah, Ill. (1990)

Most sub-par scores, fourth round

17 — at Pebble Beach (Calif.) Golf Links
(1982)

17 — at The Country Club, Brookline, Mass.
(1988)

*Most sub-par rounds by one player in one
championship*

4 — Lee Trevino, at Oak Hill C.C. (East
Course), Rochester, N.Y. (1968)

4 — Bill Casper, at The Olympic Club
(Lakeside Course), San Francisco, Calif.
(1966)

4 — Tony Jacklin, at Hazeltine National G.C.,
Chaska, Minn. (1970)

Highest score, one hole

19 — Ray Ainsley, at the 16th (par 4) at
Cherry Hills C.C., Englewood, Colo.
(1938)

Most consecutive birdies

6 — George Burns (holes 2–7), at Pebble
Beach (Calif.) Golf Links (1972)

Most consecutive 3s

7 — Hubert Green (holes 10–16), at Southern
Hills Country Club, Tulsa, Okla. (1977)

7 — Peter Jacobsen (holes 1–7), at The
Country Club, Brookline, Mass. (1988)

Most consecutive Opens

35 — Jack Nicklaus (1957-91)

Most Opens completed 72 holes

30 — Jack Nicklaus

Most consecutive Opens completed 72 holes

22 — Walter Hagen (1913-36; no Championships 1917-18)

22 — Gene Sarazen (1920-41)

22 — Gary Player (1958-79)

Writer **John Hopkins** is golf correspondent for the *Financial Times* in London, England.

Lawrence Levy is a photographer based in London, England, a contributor to many magazines and author of several books.

Rusty Jarrett is a photographer based in Martinez, Georgia.

Contributing photographer **Michael Cohen** is based in New York City.